Wovoka: The Life and Legacy of the Prophet of the Ghost Dance Movement

By Charles River Editors

Introduction

Frederic Remington's illustration of a Ghost Dance

Wovoka (1867-1932), the Ghost Dance Prophet, was a member of the Walker River band of Paiutes, in western Nevada. The Walker River Reservation was established in 1859 and was Wokova's home off and on for years. Wovoka was also known as Jack Wilson, a name he acquired while he was, for some years, employed on the David Wilson family ranch in the Mason Valley. At that time in Nevada, Indians not living on a reservation often lived on a ranch. Wovoka was exposed to the pious Wilson family's daily Bible readings, and that may have helped shape his own beliefs.

His father was a traditional medicine man, himself a devotee of an earlier prophet. In 1889, Wovoka followed his father in also becoming a medicine man. The year, Wovoka had a series of visions that led to what is sometimes called the Ghost Dance religion, which spread like wildfire across much of the West in 1889 and 1890.

"Paiute" is the common term for a number of bands who call themselves the Numu, which simply means "The People." Some tribal history is relevant to his story. There are historically three main groupings of the Paiute peoples: the Northern, the Southern and the bands in the Owens Valley. The languages of these three groups are not mutually intelligible. The various groups inhabited primarily the Great Basin region, including most of Nevada, western Utah, parts of eastern and northeastern California, and parts of Idaho, Oregon and Arizona. Wovoka was a Southern Paiute.

The Numu peoples were hunter gatherers, living on game such as rabbits, fish from rivers and lakes, and a variety of bulbs, berries, plants and nuts, particularly pinon nuts from the pinon pines. The populations were small, widely scattered and the environment was harsh. Once neighboring peoples acquired horses, some of the Paiute bands were subject to slave raids by the Utes, who sold captives to Hispanics in the Southwest and Mexico (Hanes & Hillstrom).

All three groups of Paiutes were adversely affected by settlement in the 1850s and 1860s. The American invasion of the Great Basin and the West began almost immediately after the Mexican War. The Gold Rush in California in 1849 quickly brought 200,000 outsiders to California, which became a state in 1850. Mormon settlement in Utah and the surrounding region developed before the Mexican War, from the 1840s, and the wagon trains on the Oregon Trail, also starting before the War, greatly increased.

In 1857, silver was discovered in Virginia City in western Nevada. It proved to be the richest silver strike in American history, and brought in thousands of prospectors and miners. Virginia City had 4,000 people in 1862 and grew to 25,000 by 1874. Silver was the main reason Nevada Territory was created in 1861, and Nevada silver helped finance the North during the Civil War. Gold was discovered in Colorado in 1858, which soon brought in 100,000 prospectors. These massive population influxes swamped the native peoples in their own homelands. It seems likely that the Nevada Paiutes were outnumbered by settlers and prospectors before 1860 (Digital Hist).

The rapidly increasing population of settlers quickly affected the Paiute way of life. White hunters decimated game, and cattle grazing competed with grazing wildlife. Ranchers poisoned gophers and rabbits, which had formed part of the traditional diet. A particular problem was that mines needed wooden supports for the mine shafts, and a large portion of the pinon pines in the region were cut for mine use. Nuts from the pinon pines had been one of the main food sources for the Paiute, so cutting the pines literally cut into their traditional sustenance. The name "Wovoka" means "woodcutter," so he may have cut some of the pines for sale to miners (May 19).

The different bands did not suffer quietly. There were many skirmishes as various Paiute bands raided immigrant trains, killed prospectors, and raided ranches. There were two wars with the settlers and the Army, the Snake War of 1864-66 and the Bannock War of 1878. The Bannock, based in Idaho, were related to the Paiutes. "Snakes" was a term used for various Paiute bands, with the war involving guerrilla-style skirmishes in several western states. Many of the skirmishes occurred in the Snake River basin region (the Snake is a major tributary of the Columbia River). There were more than 40 recorded Paiute skirmishes with U.S. Army and state militia groups. The end result was military defeat, and most bands being settled on a number of different reservations. Paiutes made a living as best they could, combining hunting, fishing, selling fish and game, and working as ranch hands (Hanes & Hillstrom).

Wovoka's 1889 visions grew into a new religion that gripped the hopes and imaginations of dozens of tribal groups, and it eventually extended over much of the West. It was a kind of antidote for defeat and cultural dislocation. The Lakota Sioux in particular were so caught up in the Ghost Dance and their adaptation of Wovoka's revelations that they remain strongly associated with the Ghost Dance more than a century later.

Resisting Assimilation

Prophets sometimes arose as a kind of resistance to the changes being forced on native peoples. Prophetic voices arose among several native peoples in places as far apart as New Zealand and South Africa. Almost all the prophetic voices began with the prophet experiencing a vision of visiting the Creator, being instructed in what the Creator wished for the people, and then preaching the rites, dances and other things associated with the new dispensation. Wovoka was a prophet like these.

There were some unusual tribal approaches to religion in the American West. In the Puget Sound area, a man named John Slocum of the Squaxin tribe started a sect known as the Indian Shakers. This group combined elements from Catholic and Protestant doctrine, revered Jesus as their savior, used crucifixes and the sign of the cross, but rejected the Bible. Their dances involved the kind of shaking moves that had gotten the original Shakers their name, and Slocum's group got named after the Shakers. The Indian Shakers thought their revelations were directly from Christ. There is no known connection between this sect and Wovoka, but it does indicate the variety of religious ideas (McCann 29).

Sometimes a new form of preaching from a prophet helped people adjust to the changes, and sometimes it resulted in disaster. Situations roughly comparable to the Ghost Dance existed with some of the Aborigines in Australia, the Maori in New Zealand, the Xhosa and a number of other peoples in South Africa. There were earlier prophets in the United States than Wovoka, including the Shawnee Prophet, and Handsome Lake, the important Iroquois reformer.

A common element in the prophetic voices was the belief that if the faithful sincerely performed the rites prescribed by the prophet, performed the dances and rearranged their lives according to the prophet's vision, the difficult present would be replaced with a much better future. The Creator would be moved by how faithful people were to the new revelations. Wovoka was typical in that he promised that sin would be swept away, the buffalo would come back, the ancestors would return, the dead awaken, that there would be no more disease, no more death and no more famine.

Wovoka arose in this context of unsettled peoples. His doctrines appealed to dozens of tribal groups, but each interpreted the teachings in its own way. The more desperate the tribe's situation, the more militant the Ghost Dance religion became. There was an additional problem in Wovoka getting his beliefs across to interested tribal visitors. Delegations from dozens of tribes came to see and speak with Wovoka, and the different tribes spoke different languages, and could not always understand each other (McCann 33).

The Lakota adapted Wovoka's basic prescriptions, but they added to it the disappearance of the white people, who seemed to the various Sioux tribes to be the cause of all their problems. The Lakota version of the Ghost Dance became much more militant than Wovoka's original teaching, and the Lakota version would culminate with the tragedy at Wounded Knee (Galbreath 116-117).

Many tribes suffered in the transition from tradition to reservation, but the Lakota peoples were particularly affected. They had suffered multiple reverses since being forced onto the reservations, and being forced onto the reservations was the result both of military defeat and the near annihilation of the bison herds. The Lakota once had prospered hunting bison on the high plains, building their tribal economy around the herds.

With the near extinction of the bison herds, the Lakota were reduced to accepting government rations and raising some cattle. In 1888, disease struck the Lakota livestock. In 1888 and 1889 there were crop failures. Rations promised to the tribes by treaty failed to arrive, and large amounts of land were removed from reservation status, and opened for settlement.

The reservations were also affected by disease. Whooping cough and influenza hit hard in the winter of 1889-90, taking a heavy toll of children. This may be related to Congress reducing rations supplies to the reservations by 20-25% as a cost cutting measure, which resulted in hunger (Hamalainen 377).

What the Lakota experienced was rather similar to the somewhat earlier experience of the Xhosa people in South Africa. The Xhosa, far more numerous than the Sioux, were cattle herders, and were not a horse-oriented people, like the Indians. However, like the Lakota, the Xhosa had also experienced catastrophic military defeat, massive loss of lands, their culture was denigrated and their traditions proved incapable of coping with the changes. A young prophet named Mlanjeni appeared and told the people to kill all their dun and white colored cattle.

In 1856, another prophet named Mhlakaza appeared, who had far greater influence and much more rigorous instructions. The people were told to kill all their cattle, destroy their grain and not plant crops, and follow the rituals. If they did so, the British would disappear and the world would make sense again. Many Xhosa believed that the Russians would come to save them, based on the belief that the Russians were Black, a strange belief that might have stemmed from some rumor of the Crimean War. About 20,000 Xhosa starved to death and most of the rest were impoverished. Desperate circumstances generated a desperate need to believe (Galbreath 118-119).

In New Zealand, a prophet rose among some of the Maori, a man called Te Ua Haumene. He received visions and messages from the angel Gabriel, who promised that if the new revelations were followed, the Europeans would be expelled from the islands, the dead would arise, there would be no more sickness or death, the blind would see, the lame would walk and the world would be healed, all similar to the things Wovoka promised. As with Wovoka, the message was interpreted differently by some groups, and prophecy merged into violent resistance by some of the Maori, which was put down nearly as ruthlessly as the Lakota dance (Galbraith 125).

The pressure on the Indians to change their way of life was relentless. A man named William Welsh visited the Great Sioux Reservation in South Dakota during 1880, and came to the conclusion that reservations were useless. In 1881, Welsh founded the Indian Rights Association, which did not advocate what it might sound like. The Association favored abolishing the reservations, and pushed for complete assimilation. Welsh's desire to convert the tribal people to Christianity was strong. He thought that the tribes had to be purged of pagan beliefs, taught to labor, taught civilized ways and learn to serve God (Gump 28).

The belief that Indians must become assimilated was shared by Captain Richard Henry Pratt, who, in 1879, founded the famous Indian School in Carlisle, Pennsylvania. Pratt rejected the idea of reservations entirely, arguing that reservations perpetuated superstition, savagery and socialism. In effect, views like Pratt's were that Indians had to have the tradition educated out of them (Gump 42).

The Indian Rights Association was an important lobbying organization for assimilation. It sought to have the Great Sioux Reservation broken up. In the Sioux Act of 1889, the U.S. Congress passed legislation that carved up the reservation, allocating parts to Sioux groups, and opened up the rest, more than half of it, for settlement. The Act allowed the head of a Sioux family to obtain 320 acres. The tribes reluctantly accepted the treaty. Congress slashed the beef issue for Pine Ridge by a million pounds, and in February 1890, President Harrison opened the ceded territory for settlers, before the Indians had time to file for allotments (Gump 29-30).

Originally, the Great Sioux Reservation had included virtually all the western half of South Dakota. It had been agreed to in treaties with the Lakota branch of the Sioux people. When the large reservation was broken up, five smaller reservations remained: Standing Rock, Cheyenne River, Lower Brule, Rosebud and Pine Ridge. This was still quite a large amount of land, much of which would be lost to farmers and ranchers in the future.

The Great Sioux Reservation was far too big to remain in Lakota hands. Some opposition to it came from the desire to be able to reach the Indians more quickly, which could be done if they were on small reservations in settlements. That would be more convenient for missionaries, and make it easier for agents to control Indians.

Railroad boosters had their eyes on some of the land, both for routes and for the substantial federal land subsidy given to railroads. Liberals thought that making progress for the tribes was hindered by traditions, which were easier for Indians to retain on a reservation. These stresses, and the simple desire of ranchers and farmers for the land led to Congress chopping the big reservation into smaller ones and opening up millions of acres of it for settlement (Hamalainen 377).

Agents and missionaries constantly tried to interfere with native peoples' culture, particularly anything that was thought to reflect paganism, as it was often referred to. Missionaries urged the government to forbid dances as articulations of heathenism, particularly the Sun Dance. The Sun Dance, in particular, was considered cruel and warlike, and was punishable by arrest and imprisonment.

Banning a traditional practice was not simply disapproval, because participants could be arrested by tribal police and jailed. Christianization was a main goal, although the federal government did not endorse any particular group. The government agents on reservations had a great deal of power and could compel compliance with their wishes. Agents were often appointed for political loyalty and had no experience with, or empathy for, their Indian charges. Some were conscientious and respected the Indians, and some were petty tyrants.

Both Catholics and Protestants had equal interest and equal fervor in sending missionaries to the reservations. The impact was not always negative. Missionaries taught English, reading and writing, and often helped feed and clothe their students. Some missionaries acted as advocates for the people they tried to convert.

Almost all the missionaries were interested in eliminating any aspects of tribal cultures that were considered pagan, particularly ceremonies and dancers. Mormons, numerous in the region, were equally interested in missionary activity, but were disapproved of by the federal government and were unlikely to be appointed to head Indian agencies.

In 1883, Secretary of the Interior Henry Teller introduced the Indian Religious Crimes Code that banned some Indian ceremonial activity under pain of imprisonment. This articulated the view that traditional ceremonies were primitive, pagan and sometimes immoral. The view lasted for nearly a century (Estreicher 19).

Teller

The Code allowed agents on reservations to use force, imprisonment or withholding rations in order to stop any rite or cultural practice that the agent considered to be immoral or subversive. The law set up Courts of Indian Offenses, made up of selected Indians that formed tribunals, organized by the agents. Reservations had a force of Indian Police that enforced their decisions. The effect was to drive traditions underground. A special target was the Sun Dance, but when Wovoka's Ghost Dance emerged, it too was harassed and persecuted. The agents in charge of administering a reservation had a great deal of discretion in choosing to enforce restrictions.

A typical example of interference with tribal traditions occurred in 1888, when agent H. D. Gallagher at Pine Ridge became concerned with some customs regarding death ceremonies. The tradition of some Lakota was to clip a lock of hair from a deceased family member and keep it in a packet, sometimes called a bundle, which would cause the spirit to stay for a year. At the end of the year, a celebration was held and gifts were given in honor of the deceased. Parents might give away most of their possessions to honor a deceased son. Agent Gallagher decided to forbid the practice, making it punishable by arrest (DeMallie 400).

Adhering to these traditions was a form of resistance, of maintaining being Lakota, and many agents on reservations, as well as missionaries, were determined to eradicate traditions in the effort to force the people to assimilate. The pressure to cease the activities included a literal criminalization of some of them. The appearance of Wovoka's message and his dance offered a new way and, for believers, a way to escape. The appearance of Wovoka's message also brought renewed concern among reservation agents.

This was the context for the teaching of the prophet Wovoka. Like the Lakota and other peoples, the Paiute bands were in transition from their ancient ways of living off the land by hunting, gathering, fishing and moving across their landscape. The emerging world of reservations meant dependency on rations from the government, usually given as part of an agreement to cede tribal lands. It also meant that the Paiute world also was becoming dependent on wage work.

Wovoka's Teachings and the Ghost Dance

The name of Wovoka's father is usually given as Tivibo, sometimes spelled Tavivo or Tabibo. Tivibo was a traditional medicine man and healer, and Wovoka also became a medicine man and healer. The relationship between Tivibo and the earlier prophet called Wodziwob is not clear, but Tivibo seems to have been something of a follower and may have been an important assistant and advocate. Wovoka knew about the earlier prophet and may have known him personally. That his prophecies and his concept of the dance were broadly similar to Wodziwob's is not coincidental.

Wovoka's date of birth is usually given as 1858, but it may actually have been anywhere between 1858 and 1863. His childhood name was Quoitze Ow. Many Paiute worked on ranches, and Wovoka worked for several years on the ranch of David and Abigail Wilson in the Mason Valley. He started working for the Wilsons when he was young. Some sources say he was 14 years old, and another suggests he was 8 (UM Library).

The Wilsons were deeply religious Presbyterians, and the family provided Wovoka with ample opportunity to hear readings from the Bible, prayers and conversations about religion. Wovoka stayed some years on the ranch, working as a ranch hand until he was about 18. His years at the ranch resulted in his becoming known as Jack Wilson. He was known as Wovoka to the Indians and as Jack Wilson to the settlers and ranchers. He remained friends with the family for many years, and seems to have been treated like one of the family (New World).

At least one historian has questioned whether Wovoka was influenced by the Wilson family's piety. Wovoka apparently never learned to write English or speak it well, so readings in English would have not been effective. A problem with that argument is that he spent years with the family during his adolescence and was accepted into their ranch house. He became lifetime friends with the three sons of the family, and there are stories that the three sons helped Wovoka manufacture a miracle or two. Wovoka and the eldest son seem to have become blood brothers. It seems likely he would have had to learn some English and for them to learn some Paiute for that level of friendship.

There had been another Paiute prophet, who preached his vision about 20 years before Wovoka, who also advocated a dance, a man named Wodziwob (1848-1918), who had a considerable impact on tribes in the Great Basin area. He began prophesying in 1870, and he also connected the rite of dancing with the emergence of a new world in which the dead would reappear and the whites would vanish. Wodziwob's version was an adaptation of the traditional circle dance, with a pole in the middle of the circle as a focus (May 21-22).

Wodziwob's dance is also called a Ghost Dance, but that term seems to have originated with the spread of Wovoka's version of the dance to the Lakota people and been applied to Wodziwob's dance retrospectively. His dance had a much more limited geography, mainly in Nevada and nearby areas of adjacent states. It faded considerably after prophecies about the coming cataclysm that would renew the world did not materialize, but continued among the Paiute and some tribes in California and Oregon (Bowker).

Wovoka married a woman named Tumm when he was about 20. She is also known as Mary Wilson, and their marriage lasted 50 years. They lost two sons, but raised three daughters (Ghost Dance).

Following in the steps of his father, Wovoka began to practice as a traditional medicine man and healer in the 1880s. Trances in which medicine men experienced visions were common. Paiute medicine men tended to have specialties, and Wovoka's seems to have been predicting the weather. Medicine men were more than just mystic, they also practiced traditional medicine for the sick and the injured.

On January 1st, 1889, a total solar eclipse occurred in the West, centered in Nevada and California. Wovoka went into a trance on that day, apparently in the midst of a fever. His vision was that he died from the fever and was transported to heaven. He was then reborn as a prophet with a message to take back to the native peoples (Moses 339-41).

Over time, Wovoka had many visions, and different instructions from the Creator. In one particularly vivid vision that seems to have had wide appeal, Wovoka told how God would send a 30-foot wave of new soil across the world, crushing the whites beneath its weight. If Indians danced and wore feathers in their hair, they would be lifted into the air while the new world emerged below them and submerged the whites (Johnson 44).

Wovoka began telling people about his visions and what the Creator wished the people to do. He began with the local peoples. Wovoka was repeatedly described as an impressive man, over six feet tall, with an impressive way of speaking. That doubtlessly helped him spread the word, but the content of his preaching offered something that tribes throughout the West found attractive.

The message traveled quickly and had a far wider reach than the teaching of Wodziwob. Wovoka's message and his dance traveled south to the Hualapis, north to the Shoshones and Bannocks, and east to the Caddos, Pawnees, Kiowas, Comanche and the Lakota. The story of the coming of a messiah who would bring back the buffalo, bring back the dead, rid the world of death, sickness and rid the world of white Americans had very wide appeal (Moses 341).

The theology Wovoka spread was not systematic. He was clearly influenced by Christianity, and possibly all those Bible readings in the Wilson family's home had an effect on his views. He preached that people should be at peace and not harm anyone, work hard, and be kind to one another. And they should dance. They should do a round dance, men and women together in a circle, holding hands, chanting and singing. They should dance four nights in a row ad all night on the fifth.

People from dozens of tribes responded to Wovoka's message, and most interpreted it in their own way. Most of the believers did incorporate some version of the dance. The Ghost Dance Prophet's message had the widest geographic spread of any 19th century Native American prophet, far wider than other Native American religious figures. He is certainly the most widely known.

A sort of letter from Wovoka to native peoples has survived. Called the "Messiah Letter," it was revealed by an adherent to James Mooney, a pioneering American ethnologist, who read and translated it into a kind of freeform English. It was a text written down as Wovoka spoke, written in a kind of broken English by Casper Edson, a young Arapaho listener who had gotten some education at the Carlisle School. The date of the letter is sometime in the summer of 1891, when Wovoka spoke to a number of young believers. Mooney was sympathetic to the religion, and spoke to many believers. His patience and attitude gradually led to trust. Mooney characterized Wovoka as the messiah of the religion. It's not clear, however, if Wovoka considered himself to be the messiah.

Mooney

James Mooney (1861-1921) was one of a group of pioneering ethnologists who worked for John Wesley Powell, the famous explorer of the Colorado River, who had become Director of the Smithsonian's new Bureau of American Ethnology. The group was notable for its sympathy with the tribal peoples, and the researchers spent a lot of time with the tribal people, learning languages and reporting what they learned. The Bureau essentially created the discipline of ethnology, and the information they collected and published forms an extremely important source for American Indians in the era. Mooney himself was not particularly well educated, but his reports remain useful after more than a century.

Mooney interviewed Wovoka in 1892. He told Mooney details of his visions, of God sharing with him the vision of a new world full of game and he was given a view of his ancestors. Much as in the Messiah Letter, he told Mooney that people should not lie, should not steal, should work, and should not make war (New World).

Mooney had spent a lot of time with various tribal groups and was trusted by all of them. An Indian gave Mooney the letter because they trusted him to tell the truth about the religion.

Mooney commented that they gave him the letter to show that there was nothing bad or hostile in their religion, and they wanted him to take the letter to Washington to prove that the religion was peaceful.

The letter contains instructions for acolytes. They were told that when they got home, they must "make a dance to continue for five days. Dance four successive days and on the fifth day keep the dance up until the morning of the fifth day, when all must bathe in the river and then disperse to their homes" (Mooney).

Wovoka said that he would send believers a good cloud which would make them feel good, and he gave them a good spirit and give them good paint. The cloud probably refers to rain, and the paint to decorations for dancers, such as red ochre. He asked them to return to him in three months. He promised heavy rain in the fall and a lot of snow (Mooney).

In the letter, Wovoka said, "Grandfather says when your friends die, you must not cry. You must not hurt anybody or do harm to anyone. Do right always, it will give you satisfaction in life." Wovoka said not to tell the white people, but Jesus was back on the Earth, and that he will appear like a cloud. The dead were coming alive, and Wovoka thought they might appear in the coming fall or spring. When the future comes, said Wovoka, there will be no more sickness and everyone will be young again (Mooney).

He also told them to work for the whites and not to make any trouble with them until leaving them. He said that when the world shakes at the coming of the new world, do not be afraid because believers would not be hurt. He also told them to hold a dance every six weeks, and to make a feast at the dance and have enough for everyone to eat. Then they were to bathe in the water. He would send good words again at some unspecified time (Mooney).

Wovoka's vision was not of a far distant future. He told the believers that the messiah would come soon, maybe in the spring of 1891. That prediction gave the dances a particular intensity.

There is one interpretation of Wovoka's prophecies that asserts that he had two separate messages, one for the Indians and another for whites, so that the whites would not fear what Wovoka was saying. The version for whites was that his prediction of the coming new world was actually in the other world, after life on Earth. The version for Indians was that the new world would occur after a cataclysm in this world, which would crush the whites (Bowker).

Wovoka's dance was quickly taken up by tribes all across the West. The pattern of traditional peoples caught up in a maelstrom of change forced upon them was common in the middle to late 1800s. Peoples were losing their land, their independence was being limited, and their culture forced to change. Traditions no longer seemed adequate to cope with the magnitude of the changes forced upon them, so Wovoka's optimistic teachings were welcome.

The dance Wovoka prescribed was a kind of round dance, the dancers forming a circle, with fingers interlocked. In the known Ghost Dances, there was none of the usual accompaniment of drums and rattles, only singing. The dance itself was a kind of circular shuffle, simply an adaptation of a traditional dance form. Dancers would start in the evening, and chant and sing for hours.

The effect seems often to have been almost hypnotic, with dancers sometimes literally falling down into a trance. People waking from the trance would be eagerly questioned about their visions. What they often reported often was seeing dead loved ones and a sense that a purer world that would come soon. What they saw was often the return of the buffalo and the vanishing of the white people (Johnson 45).

Lakota delegates had visited Wovoka in Nevada in early 1890, and returned home as converts. They apparently traveled by train to reach the place and return. The Lakota visitors included men named Kicking Bear and Short Bull. Kicking Bear began preaching on Wovoka's doctrine at the Standing Rock and Cheyenne River reservations. He was instrumental in introducing the dance to the Lakota. One aspect that especially interested the Lakota was the return of ancestors to the Earth, of spirits joining them and the dead rejoining their families and communities (Gump 34).

Kicking Bear spoke with Wovoka, listened to the prophet's descriptions of his visions, and also experienced his own visions, in which the Creator spoke to him directly. Kicking Bear's visions were generally similar to Wovoka's, but were harsher on the whites. It's not clear if Kicking Bear regarded himself as a fellow prophet, or as a disciple of Wovoka's. Kicking Bear preached on the Cheyenne River reservation and then moved on to Standing Rock. There was no secret about the new faith, and both settlers and reservation officials knew about it almost as soon as it started. On October 22, the Deadwood *Black Hills Daily Times* reported that the "Messiah craze" had reached Standing Rock (DeMontravel 26).

Kicking Bear described how that when the Creator spread new Earth over the landscape, that dancers who kept dancing would stamp down the new soil as they danced, rising as the new Earth was being spread beneath their feet, burying settlers and soldiers. Wovoka had said that the dancers should wear feathers in their hair which would lift them into the air as the new surface appeared and covered the old world. Kicking Bear doesn't seem to have preached that detail.

Lakota interpretation of Wovoka's message emphasized that the dead would return and join the living. It is unknown whether the trances that some dancers experienced always involved visions of the ancestors and the recently dead, but the visions contained the sense of the ancestors returning, so they called Wovoka's circle dance the "spirit dance." "Spirit Dance" was changed by whites to "Ghost Dance," the name it has been called ever since (Warren 665).

Many Lakota and members of other groups viewed Wovoka as not just a prophet, but as the Messiah, the literal second coming of Jesus. Many Indians believed that the first time Jesus had come to Earth, he wanted to help the white people, but instead of being grateful and accepting his help and listening to him, the white people killed him. The Lakota and others had been exposed to missionaries, and had heard the biblical stories about Jesus and the crucifixion, but sometimes interpreted it in a way the missionaries did not imagine.

Some of the believers thought that this time around, Jesus would wipe the unbelieving whites off the face of the Earth, and usher in a new age in which the Indians would emerge as the chosen people. Many of the believers thought that the new millennium would come in the spring of 1891, so for them the dances had a special importance and fervor (Jacoby 336).

The Lakota were far from unified in their beliefs about the Ghost Dance. The Oglala leader, American Horse. criticized the ghost dancers as dangerous and said that dancers visiting from the Rosebud reservation had destroyed property. The dancers alienated many traditionalists like American Horse, and alienated many of the more progressive members of the tribe. Still, it appealed to thousands of Lakota, who became adherents and joined in the dancing and rituals (Gump 35).

The ghost shirt that has ever since been associated with the Ghost Dance was a Lakota innovation, apparently invented in June of 1890. It was made from buckskin, muslin or whatever material was available, usually fringed, and the owner might paint a variety of symbols on it. The symbols might be moons and stars or include things of particular sacredness to that individual and spoke to the concerns of each dancer. Every ghost shirt was different, and the shirts were worn by both men and women during the dance, although not every dancer wore one.

Women joining in the dance with men was an innovation in Lakota culture, but accepted by the dancers. The idea that the ghost shirt would stop the soldier's bullets was also a Lakota development, although it is not clear how widespread that belief was or just how it originated (Johnson 45).

Kicking Bear seems to have been the one who converted Sitting Bull, which was critical for the dance because of Sitting Bull's immense prestige as a leader. He was an aging man, and it is not known if he actually joined the dancers (Johnson 44).

Kicking Bear

Sitting Bull

Sitting Bull's approval of Wovoka's prophecies gave prestige and authority to the new religion and to the dance. His prestige and his endorsement of the dance was seen as a major problem by James McLaughlin, agent at the Standing Rock reservation, who had a strong dislike of the chief. McLaughlin called the dance "an absurd craze," and he further described it as "demoralizing, indecent and disgusting." This agent's view of Sitting Bull as an obstruction to what he saw as progress was to have fateful results (Reilly 7-8).

Another convert to Wovoka's dance was the Lakota Short Bull. Short Bull assured his followers that if they sang a song he taught them, and they had to confront soldiers, that some of the soldiers would drop dead and the rest would start to run but would sink into the Earth and all the soldiers and whites would fall dead. That was far from Wovoka's actual message, but it appealed to many Lakota, perhaps because the Lakota's wars with the soldiers and defeat was more recent than that of the Paiutes.

Short Bull was not advocating any form of violence. God would get rid of the whites, he thought, not war from the Indians. In the coming world, native people would have the wisdom and the power. There doesn't seem to be any consistency in the view of where white people would fit in this world. In some versions, the white people simply vanish, swallowed up by the Earth. Some thought that they would trade places, with the whites becoming helpless and powerless (DeMallie 394-5).

The largest group of Ghost Dancers camped in a portion of the Badlands northwest of the Pine Ridge agency. Doing so means they were away from the prying eyes of the agent and his employees, but it also would have aroused suspicion that they were up to something no good (Reilly 7).

By the late fall of 1890, the Ghost Dance had become national news. A recent study of coverage of the Ghost Dance in the two Omaha and Nebraska newspapers illustrates the different kinds of coverage the dance received. The *World Herald* was moderate, and criticized the administration of the reservations for being harsh. The *Bee* was much more opinionated, and tended to sensationalize events, which sold newspapers (Reilly 9).

Troop trains left Omaha on November 18th as part of the mobilization that sent troops to all of the Sioux reservations. Overall, the troop mobilization was the largest since the Civil War. A reporter from the Omaha *Bee* accompanied the troops, and his stories focused on intrigue and violence, and claimed that Lakota anger was seething at Pine Ridge. His reports were reprinted all across the country, and contributed to the view that the Ghost Dance was becoming a threat to public safety. To an extent, this kind of sensationalistic coverage shaped the violence that was soon to follow (Reilly 9).

Ghost Dance Apocalypse

The essence of what happened with the Ghost Dance and the Lakota is that it was another attempt to get rid of the white people increasingly infringing on Lakota life and land. The Lakota tried war for a generation, from the 1850s through the 1870s, and it worked for a time. They lost militarily, and with the demise of the buffalo herds, reservations were basically the last refuge. Sitting Bull had taken some Lakota to exile in Canada, but eventually returned - the Canadian government considered them American Indians and not a Canadian responsibility.

Wovoka's new religion promised a new way, a coming of a new age in which the Creator would cause the buffalo to return and the white people would be swept away. It had a huge appeal to many Lakota, who, for a few months from late summer to early winter of 1890, reveled in their interpretation of Wovoka's teachings, and thousands of Lakota enthusiastically joined in the Ghost Dancing (DeMallie 392).

Reservation agents, settlers and others quickly picked up on the fervency of the Ghost Dance believers, but interpreted it as something like a war dance, and not a religious rite. They interpreted the Ghost Dance as a kind of vehicle for Lakota anger and thought it might be whipping up sentiment for violence. Different groups of Lakota interpreted the dance and Wovoka's message in various ways. Some bands were aware that the whites were getting upset. Fearing a U.S. Army attack, several groups went to remote areas to set up Ghost Dance camps. Although smaller than they had been, the reservations were large enough to have remote area where dancing could be unobserved (DeMallie 387-88).

The Sioux tribes had long had a reputation for being formidable warriors and for hostility to whites. In 1862, there had been a grimly violent uprising in Minnesota that killed 800 settlers and had been promptly and violently repressed. When told that hungry Indians asked for food, one agent had said "Let them eat grass." He was found dead with his mouth stuffed with grass.

Called the "Dakota Uprising," it had begun with restlessness on reservations. Perhaps 1,500 Indians died in the fighting and the subsequent repression. 38 of the so-called rebels were hanged at Mankato, Minnesota in December 1862 as part a mass execution. Agents and settlers in 1890 clearly remembered that episode of extreme violence and that it was related to restlessness among Sioux tribes.

In the fall of 1890, the War Department sent troops to all of the Lakota reservations. Troops were sent to Pine Ridge and Rosebud, and they were also posted outside Standing Rock and Cheyenne River. Just why they did so is not clear. At one time it was thought that settlers had panicked because of the Ghost Dance and fled to towns, begging for the protection of soldiers, but that appears not to have been the case. Historians have investigated that possibility and concluded that there was no settler or rancher panic (Ostler 220-21).

There were other factors at work as well. Deploying 7,000 soldiers, a quarter of the entire U.S. Army, on or near the Lakota reservations might seem to be an overreaction, but politics entered the situation. President Benjamin Harrison regarded South Dakota as an important state, and voters during the next election would appreciate the government deploying troops (Hamalainen 378).

An ongoing problem was the quality of the agents appointed to the reservations. In October 1890, Daniel Royer was appointed agent at Pine Ridge, apparently as a reward for services rendered to the Republican party of South Dakota. He had no experience whatsoever working with native people and little, if any, understanding of, or respect for, Lakota culture. Worried about the Ghost Dance, he asked for troops, and on November 15th, the Acting Director of Indian Affairs told the President that Pine Ridge needed the presence of the Army. President Benjamin Harrison authorized the use of troops (Ostler 227).

Royer seems to have known little about the desperation of the Indians whose lives he was overseeing. He wrote, "Indians are dancing in the snow and are wild and crazy…We need protection and we need it now" (Jacoby 336).

There was another kind of politics at work. In 1849, Indian Affairs had been transferred from the Department of War to the new Department of the Interior. This seems to have started a bureaucratic rivalry, with Army officers thinking that civilian agents were often incapable of dealing with Indians. The trend of thought was that Army officers with experience in the West knew Indians and were more capable of dealing with them than inexperienced political appointees.

In the 1880s and 1890s, the U.S. Army was being modernized, and changing from being largely a guardian of the frontier against hostile tribes. The Army bureaucracy in the West saw itself as vital, and so the Ghost Dance represented an opportunity for the Army to justify its importance. On November 17th, General Nelson Miles noted in the Dakota region there were 1,400 mounted soldiers, and 30,000 disaffected Indians with 6,000 warriors. His recommendation was that more troops were needed there (Ostler 235).

Miles

Miles warned of a possible Indian war and implied that it might be the most serious ever. He may or may not have been intentionally exaggerating the threat, but he seems to have used the Ghost Dance as evidence that something threatening was happening. The extent of the Ghost Dance in 1890 is not known, although historians think it might have been only 4,000 dedicated dancers among the 20,000 Lakota. It is possible General Miles wanted to make his name better known, as he was an ambitious man and may have been considering a presidential run in 1892 (Warren 666).

Miles may or may not have believed in actual the possibility of an insurrection, but he does seem to have thought that a massive buildup of troops would overawe the Indians. The buildup would also justify the importance of the Army in the West and help the Army in claiming an expanded role in Indian affairs. It would also calm any concerns that settlers had about an Indian uprising (Ostler 239).

There was a serious outbreak of violence on December 15th, two weeks before the tragedy at Wounded Knee. Sitting Bull was the most influential Lakota chief and had surrendered in 1881. For almost two years was kept a prisoner at Ft. Randall on the Missouri river. Sitting Bull was apparently enthusiastic about what he had heard of Wovoka, and he endorsed the Ghost Dance. The reservation agent regarded Sitting Bull as a stubborn obstacle who kept getting in the way of the agent's policies for the Indians. Removing Sitting Bull would make life easier for the agent and, it was hoped, defuse the Ghost Dance (Hamalainen 374).

Standing Rock agent McLaughlin sent a force of 43 Indian police to bring in Sitting Bull. The Indian Police provided the muscle for a reservation's agent to enforce his views. They also represented a division within the tribe between traditionalists and others. The police arrived at Sitting Bull's camp, which consisted of two cabins, just before 6:00 in the morning. Their intent was to arrest him so that he could be detained in the reservation jail. That the agent sent 43 police to arrest one man suggests that trouble was expected.

The police raided both cabins. Initially, Sitting Bull appears to have been cooperating, but began to struggle, and violence followed. One of the chief's followers, Catch the Bear, shot Bull Head, one of the police. A firefight erupted, killing Sitting Bull, his teenage son Crow Foot, and six other Sitting Bull supporters. Six of the police were also killed (Jacoby 337).

The remaining police were surrounded by angry supporters of Sitting Bull. It took a cavalry detachment to extricate them and calm the violence. McLaughlin had arranged for Army backup for his force of Indian police, two troops of cavalry equipped with both a Gatling gun and a Hotchkiss gun. The soldiers intervened and quieted the rage. The bodies were tossed in a wagon, taken to Ft. Yates, just across the border into North Dakota, and buried there without ceremony (Markley).

This incident left 14 people dead and polarized the Lakota even more. It also made national news and turned public opinion against the Ghost Dance. In the late summer, the public view of the Ghost Dance seems to have been that it was harmless, a view that changed to seeing the Ghost Dance as a dangerous kind of militancy. Before the Sitting Bull incident, there had been no actual violence associated with the dance (Reilly 14).

A number of Sitting Bull's followers fled to the camp of a chief named Big Foot (who was also called Spotted Elk) where they thought they would find safety. The Army assumed that Big Foot was Sitting Bull's successor and considered them hostile. In reality, Sitting Bull was a very influential chief, but not the actual head of a tribe and had no successor. Big Foot decided to move his band of about 350 to the Pine Ridge reservation. In a few weeks, they would camp at a place called Wounded Knee Creek (Hamalainen 378).

There had been another plan to remove Sitting Bull from the reservation without killing him. Had the other way succeeded, Wounded Knee might have been avoided. In 1885, the chief had spent several months as a main attraction of Buffalo Bill's famous Wild West Show, traveling with the show, being well paid for his participation, and becoming friends with Buffalo Bill Cody. Sitting Bull apparently trusted Cody (DeMontravel 29-31).

This highly improbable, but true story began with General Miles telegraphing Cody, asking him to come to South Dakota and go to the Standing Rock reservation to "secure the person" of Sitting Bull. Miles asked Buffalo Bill to deliver Sitting Bull to the nearest commanding Army officer, apparently assuming their friendship would make the chief more amenable to surrendering. Cody was just back from touring Europe and was scheduled to testify before a Congressional committee. Cody was not just a showman - he had been a scout for the Army and a soldier. In 1890, Cody was a private citizen, and Miles had no legal authority to command a private citizen to apprehend an Indian chief on a reservation, but Cody obliged (Stillman).

Buffalo Bill

Cody recruited three friends, all members of the Wild West Show, and they arrived by train at Mandan, South Dakota on November 27th. Cody telegraphed agent McLaughlin that they had arrived and would proceed to the reservation to try to persuade Sitting Bull to go with them. McLaughlin was opposed to the effort, which perhaps could indicate that the agent was planning on getting rid of the recalcitrant chief himself. McLaughlin managed to put enough obstacles in Cody's way so that he never got to see Sitting Bull. Cody reached the reservation center on the 28th and was told the Chief was visiting elsewhere.

The following day, the story goes, Cody was dead drunk and in no condition to travel, and apparently agent McLaughlin's men had plied him with the liquor. The day after that, having since sobered up, Cody obtained a couple of wagons, in which he and his three friends, as well as five newspaper reporters, were going to ride to visit Sitting Bull. They had brought with them a large supply of sweets, because the chief was fond of candy. The presence of five reporters was a typical Cody touch, because he had learned the value of publicity from his Wild West Show.

This strange twist in the story ended when they got a telegram from President Harrison countermanding General Miles' original instructions. Cody and friends left, returning home. There was no meeting between Buffalo Bill and Sitting Bull that might have helped ease the tensions on the reservation. There is no way of knowing if the chief would have peaceably gone with Buffalo Bill, but if he had done so, it might have defused the coming confrontation (Stillman).

A sizable band of Ghost Dancers and others led by the Minneconjou chief Big Foot, left a camp and wanted to find refuge at the Pine Ridge agency. The weather was bitter cold, and Indians were fearful of the Army. The band consisted of about 350 Lakota, from several bands, and included about 120 men and 230 women and children (Reilly 16).

It was a coincidence that the troops belonged to the 7th Cavalry, the same regiment that the Sioux had almost annihilated at the Battle of the Little Big Horn back in 1876. It is unknown if the troops saw Wounded Knee as an opportunity to take revenge for Custer and his men. Some historians make that claim. The now-dead Sitting Bull had been one of the chiefs leading the Lakota and their allies in that battle. The troops certainly would have known that.

Officers thought that Big Foot's group was armed and that their participation in the Ghost Dance was proof they were probably hostile. The Army saw the Ghost Dance not as a religious rite but as a war dance. Some of the men in Big Foot's group did own guns (Reilly 16-17).

A detachment of the 7th Cavalry caught up with the band, which surrendered. They were escorted to a place on Wounded Knee creek, where they set up a camp. The group was surrounded by soldiers. The highest-ranking officer present, Colonel James Forsythe, took command of the situation. On the morning of December 29th, another bitterly cold day, Forsythe detailed two companies to disarm the Indians. That meant that soldiers and Indians became closely intermixed as the soldier searched for weapons (DeMontravel 33).

Big Foot wanted the band to obey the soldiers, so violence was not inevitable, but everyone seemed to be on edge. One version of how the violence began is that a deaf man did not understand what a soldier wanted, and fired his gun, starting a shootout. Another is that a man insisted on being paid for his rifle before he gave it to a soldier, and in the struggle, the gun fired. The initial shot resulted in a bloody melee, and the Army had devastating firepower because Forsythe had stationed a battery of four Hotchkiss guns on a hill near the encampment. Some of the soldiers had been drinking the night before.

The shooting only lasted a few minutes, and almost all of Big Foot's band was shot down, as were a number of soldiers. Women and children scattered, with the men trying to cover them, but most of the men were quickly killed. Scores of the Indians had taken refuge in a ravine nearby, but the rapid-fire Hotchkiss guns rained shells on them, killing many.

The number of Lakota killed at Wounded Knee will probably never be known. A civilian contractor billed the government $292 for burying 146 Indians, at $2 per body. Some bodies were removed during the three days from the end of the shooting to the burial details, and it is known that some of the wounded later died. A blizzard made collecting the bodies impossible for several days. It is also probable that some of the killed were never found (DeMontravel 36).

The casualties are simply estimates. Most estimates state that at least 150 were killed, but estimates range as high as 300. The soldiers were too well armed for their own good. The 7th Cavalry suffered 25 killed and 39 wounded, some killed by Indians firing back, but most of these substantial casualties were apparently killed by friendly fire. (Reilly 18).

The bodies of the Indians were buried in mass graves three days later. Several of the surviving photographs of Wounded Knee's aftermath show some of the Indians killed to be in contorted and unnatural positions, which was due to the below zero temperatures freezing their bodies. Whether Wounded Knee was a battle or a massacre is hotly contested by historians. The military thought it was a battle, and 32 of the soldiers who participated that day were awarded medals. 20 of those were Medals of Honor.

Many of the Wounded Knee dead were buried half naked because some of the soldiers stripped the ghost shirts off the corpses as souvenirs (Johnson 50).

Decades later, a first-hand account of the incident emerged when a donor gave it to the Princeton University Library. The author was a soldier named John Comfort, who was an older soldier, a veteran of fighting the Comanche in 1874, and who had won a medal of Honor in that fighting. He died in 1894, so the account was written when the memory was relatively fresh.

Comfort wrote about the Ghost Dance, "The Messiah craze and Ghost dancing had got them to believe that the Soldier's bullets would not kill them." He also wrote that the Indian medicine man had preached a "wild fanatical sermon" and said that the soldiers would kill the Indians as soon as they put their hands up and had urged them to die fighting like warriors (Jacoby 353).

Comfort acknowledged that women and children were killed, but he claimed that it was unavoidable because the warriors were mixed with them. He said that some of the Indians were "playing possum," presumably meaning pretending to be wounded or dead, then shooting at soldiers. Comfort claimed he admired the natives, writing, "Physically, they were the finest lot of men that I ever saw" (Jacoby 354).

Wounded Knee was not the last of the violence. Comfort describes patrols going out and skirmishing with small groups of Indians, with casualties on both sides. The deadly Hotchkiss guns got further use, and more troops were called in. Comfort describes the arrival of some units of the 9th Cavalry, which he called "Negro soldiers," referring to one of the regiments of the famed Buffalo Soldiers (Jacoby 356).

The incidents following Wounded Knee were small and tailed off. A few soldiers were wounded and several Lakota were killed. Wovoka's new religion and the Ghost Dance did not die at Wounded Knee, but many, perhaps most of the Lakota believers lost their faith.

After Wounded Knee

An obvious question to ask is why Wovoka himself was never arrested and imprisoned, because his association with the Ghost Dance was widely known, and he was thought by some to be preaching rebellion. Just days after Wounded Knee, local newspapers in Nevada were editorializing the concern that Indians in the state might rise up like the Lakota had in South Dakota.

The agent at the nearby Pyramid Lake reservation, C.C. Warner, said he would not give Wovoka the notoriety that arresting him would bring. He explained, "I am pursuing the course with him of nonattention." He felt that simply ignoring Wovoka was more effective at defusing the Ghost Dance than the renewed attention that arresting Wovoka would bring. Warner felt that the Ghost Dance religion was an evil influence, but in 1893 he said the "fanaticism" was over, and that the strongest weapon to use against it was ridicule. The Army left him alone and local authorities did the same (GhostDance).

General Miles had been concerned about possible violence and wanted the Ghost Dance suppressed, but he was angered by the deadly confrontation that resulted. He did not think the use of deadly force was necessary. Miles relieved Colonel Forsythe of his command, and set up a court of inquiry to investigate the incident. This could have resulted in a dishonorable discharge, which seems to have been Miles' intent. However, Forsythe was quickly absolved and quickly reinstated to his command, apparently with a nudge from President Harrison (DeMontravel 34-5).

The events at Wounded Knee became immediately controversial on a national level and have remained that way ever since. General Miles had thought that the Ghost Dance religion was cover for a planned uprising and seems to have really thought he was acting to prevent an Indian war. Nonetheless, he was something of an advocate for the Indians once danger of the Ghost Dance appeared to be gone. Miles persuaded a number of Lakotas to return to their agencies, and once they had returned, he was successful in pushing for improved rations. He bought them hundreds of pounds of coffee and sugar, and thousands of pounds of flour. The Lakota trusted him to keep his word, based on past experiences (DeMontravel 39-41).

The detachments of the 7th Cavalry that did the shooting at Wounded Knee had four Hotchkiss guns, a kind of light artillery, breech-loading and capable of rapid fire. The guns fired a 1.65 inch shell, and had recently been adopted by the Army to replace a much older version of mountain artillery. The guns were designed to be light enough to travel with cavalry units and to be usable in rough terrain. At Wounded Knee, they proved deadly.

The Hotchkiss guns have confused some researchers, historians, and commentators. A frequent claim is that the Lakota and Wounded Knee were killed by modern machine guns. However, the Hotchkiss guns at Wounded Knee were rapid fire light artillery, not machine guns. Hotchkiss, an American inventor, had a factory in France and the machine guns with his name on them were first used by the French in the 1890s, and improved versions were common weapons in the First World War.

The fact that 20 of the soldiers participating in the slaughter were awarded Medals of Honor is puzzling, because the medal was ordinarily awarded one or two at a time for acts of conspicuous bravery. Awarding 20 of them at the same time for the same engagement was highly unusual. One possibility is that the medal was normally awarded for conspicuous gallantry in combat, and the awards could be interpreted as indications that it was a real and hard-fought battle. The medals have since then become part of the controversy, and there is a movement trying to get the President to revoke all of them.

After Wounded Knee, there were all sorts of theories about the cause and about the origin of Wovoka's doctrines. One of the common theories at the time was that the Mormons were somehow the instigators. Adherents of the Church of Latter-Day Saints, popularly called Mormons, fled savage repression in the Midwest and found their homeland in the Great Basin country, now Utah.

The Mormon presence in the Great Basin region grew steadily from the 1840s on, and they started settlements over a rather wide area. They fought some Indians, took others on as ranch hands and herders, and were genuinely concerned with the Indians' spirituality. Mormon theology regarding the native peoples is complicated but saw them as biblical people and as potential converts. Mainstream opinion of the Mormons at the time was generally quite negative.

General Miles spoke to a group of newspaper reporters in St. Paul, Minnesota, in early November 1890 and said that he thought Mormons might be behind the Ghost Dance movement. In January 1891, the general wrote an essay in the widely read *North American Review*. His essay placed some blame on the Indian Affairs bureaucracy for putting the tribes on areas too small to sustain them, but also mentioned the Mormons. He blamed the Mormons for telling Indians that an Indian messiah had appeared (Smoak 269-70).

It is possible that Wovoka had some knowledge of Mormon doctrine. The faith had success in the 1870s in converting hundreds of Indians, notably some Shoshone people in the Utah-Idaho border region. There was speculation that a garment used in Mormon ritual might be the origin of the ghost shirt idea, and that the Mormon history of their prophet Joseph Smith might somehow have found an echo in a Paiute prophet (Smoak 279-82).

It is widely thought that Wounded Knee ended the Ghost Dance and ended Wovoka's role as prophet, but the dance did continue to quietly survive in some places, seemingly as a combination of belief and quiet resistance. Since it continued to exist, believers had accepted that the promised coming of the messiah in the spring of 1891 had not occurred. In 1914, the Pawnee argued that the Ghost Dance was really Christian in nature. They were granted permission to dance by Methodist and Baptist ministers, with the condition that the ministers were present and had the opportunity to speak to the assembled groups (Estreicher 20).

The Ghost Dance survived, on a diminished level, at least into the 1950s with some of the Lakota people in Canada, and with some of the Wind River Shoshone. The original prediction that the new world was coming soon was abandoned, and instead, these practitioners of the dance saw the prophecy as coming at some unknown date in the future (Bowker).

Wovoka lived more than 40 years past Wounded Knee, and for a time, he was nationally famous. There were attempts to bring him to the 1893 Columbian Exposition in Chicago, and a fair in San Francisco in 1904, both unsuccessful. The intent seems to have been to cash in on his notoriety the way that Buffalo Bill's Wild West Show had used Sitting Bull's notoriety, which was based on the massacre of Custer and his men at the Little Big Horn (GhostDance).

With the help of a white friend named E.A. Dyer, Sr., Wovoka made a something of a living by selling ritual items and personal mementos. Dyer was a storekeeper in Yearington, Nevada. Wovoka got a steady stream of letters and other requests for things he had worn, especially hats. He knew some English, but apparently could not write in English, or read it well, so Dyer was a kind of scribe for him. Wovoka asked $20 for a hat that he had worn and sold a few of them. Wovoka also did a good deal of traveling to reservations in a number of states, staying on them as a guest for as long as six months. He was sometimes given gifts of money, on one of his trips being given $1,200. Nonetheless, he continued to live a modest life in a rough two-room cabin (GhostDance).

Dyer much later wrote a short account of his experience with Wovoka. The exact date of the account is unknown, but it was sometime in the 1950s and titled "Wizardry." The account is generally friendly to Wovoka, but it describes several incidents which his followers thought were miracles as simple tricks. In one, Wovoka made ice fall from the sky, and Dyer says it was simply hidden in the branches of a tree and fell to the ground. That said, Dyer does not present Wovoka as a trickster or a fraud (Smoak 285). Dyer seems to have been a friend and a kind of business partner of Wovoka, in the business of Ghost Dance memorabilia. This traffic in Ghost Dance materials and objects associated with Wovoka was criticized at the time as evidence that he was a charlatan, making money from the faithful. However, Wovoka seems to have remained convinced of his vision, deferring the arrival of the promised new world until the Creator was ready (Moses 333-34).

The selling of Ghost Dance and Wovoka memorabilia is easy to criticize, particularly when Dyer points out details like the red ocher some of Wovoka's believers requested was shopped to them was resealed in used tomato soup cans. It's possible that Wovoka was a charlatan by this time, but it's more likely that it was simply an exchange of the traditional kind, in a new guise. Medicine men had always expected gifts for their services, and Wovoka sending a hat that he had worn is the same kind of exchange. Wovoka is reported to have made something like $35 a week from these exchanges. That would have been enough to insulate him from the poverty common on the reservations (Dangberg 13-15).

After Wounded Knee, Wovoka continued residing on the reservation. The Walker River reservation lost 206,000 acres in 1906, and most of the various Paiute band reservations and reserves lost land, and also lost water access. The reservations themselves were subject to illegal cattle grazing by outside ranchers, as well as the poaching of fish and game. It's no wonder that the Ghost Dance became a quiet form of resistance for many years, although not much is known about it (Hanes & Hillstrom).

Many Indians continued to have reverence for Wovoka. In 1924, a popular actor and director named Tim McCoy invited Wovoka to the site in northern California where he was filming a movie. McCoy had hired a number of Arapahos as helpers and extras, and they showed great reverence for the old prophet (GhostDance).

An Arapaho ghost shirt

Tim McCoy (1891-1978) was a very prominent early actor in Western movies, a director and something of a scholar of Indian life. He was noted as an advocate for the native peoples, and Wovoka's 1924 appearance was not the only association between the two. There is a popular photograph of the two, taken on the reservation in 1926, although the context of the photograph does not seem to be known.

Another twist in the Wovoka story is that one of his grandsons became a U.S. Army pilot and served with Chennault's famous Flying Tigers in the China theater of World War II. He was shot down and killed in combat with the Japanese.

Sitting Bull remains one of the best known of all Native Americans. Anything connected with him draws attention. In the 1950s, some of his descendants sought to have his grave moved from its location just over the border in North Dakota to a more appropriate spot in South Dakota. Perhaps seeing some potential tourist dollars, North Dakota objected, and even Montana asked for the body to be buried at the Little Big Horn battleground park. His grave was moved to where the descendants wished. Since then, it has been vandalized and repaired (Markley).

Wounded Knee seared the Ghost Dance into American memory. Activist Indians in the American Indian Movement, or AIM, occupied the hamlet of Wounded Knee in 1973, resulting in a months-long confrontation between natives and federal agents. Both sides were armed, and the local, state and federal force had armored cars and sharpshooters. For a time, there was the possibility of another bloodbath at Wounded Knee, but eventually anger lessened and negotiation ended the standoff. Following the incident, the FBI arrested about 1,200 people all over the country, but most were not convicted on any charges.

There were several deaths in the confrontation, although it ended peaceably. Bringing back the Ghost Dance was part of the incident, and it retains a powerful association with Wounded Knee. The Ghost Dance is still being performed, and Wovoka's message has not been forgotten.

Online Resources

Other books about Native American history by Charles River Editors

Other books about Wovoka on Amazon

Further Reading

Bowker, John. "Ghost Dance." Encyclopedia.com. encyclopedia.com/history/united-states-and-Canada/north-american-indigenous-peoples/ghost-dance/. Accessed January 12, 2022.

Dangberg, Grace. "Wovoka." *Nevada Historical Society Quarterly* 11 (2), Summer 1968. 5-56.

DeMallie, Raymond. "The Lakota Ghost Dance: An Ethnohistoric Account." *Pacific Historical Review* 51 (4), November 1982. 385-405.

DeMontravel, Peter. "General Nelson Miles and the Wounded Knee Controversy.*" Arizona and the West* 128 (1), Spring 1986. 23-44.

Digital History. "The Comstock Lode and the Mining Frontier." digitalhistory.uh.edu/. Accessed January 8, 2022.

Estreicher, Justin. " 'The Promises They Heard He Had Made': The Ghost Dance, Wounded Knee and Assimilation Through Christian Orthodoxy." Penn History Review 24 (2), April 2019. 10-23. repository.upenn.edu/phr/vol24/iss2/2/. Accessed January 6, 2022.

Galbreath, John. "Appeals to the Supernatural: Africa and New Zealand Comparisons With the Ghost Dance. *Pacific Historical Review* 57 (2), May 1982. 115-33.

GhostDance.US. "Wovoka Biography." ghostdance.us/history/history-wovokaewb.html/. Accessed January 12, 2022.

Gump, James. "A Spirit of Resistance: Sioux, Xhosa, and Maori Resistance to Western Dominance, 1840-1920." *Pacific Historical Review* 66 (1), February 1997. 21-52.

Hamalainen, Pekka. *Lakota America*. New Haven: Yale University Press, 2019.

Hanes, Richard, and Laurie Hillstrom. "Paiutes." Countries and Their Cultures. everyculture.com /multi/Le-Pa/Paiutes.html/. Accessed January 8, 2022.

Jacoby, Karl. "Of Memory and Massacre: A Soldier's Firsthand Account of the 'Affair on Wounded Knee.' "

Johnson, Dorothy. "Ghost Dance: Last Hope of the Sioux." *Montana, The Magazine of Western History* 6 (3), Summer 1956. 42-50.

Kerstetter, Todd. "Ghost Dance." *Encyclopedia of the Great Plains.* plainshumanities.uni.edu/encyclopedia/doc/egp.rel.023/. Accessed January 11, 2022.

Markley, Bill. "Sitting Bull Rests, But Is He at Peace?" History.net. historynet.com/sitting-bull-rests-peace.htm/. Accessed January 13, 2022.

May, Alexander. *The Reconstructive Power of Wovoka's Prophetic Discourse. A Rhetorical Analysis of the 1890 Ghost Dance Prophet*. Thesis, University of Nevada, 2004. Digitalscholarship.unv.edu/cgi/viewcontent/. Accessed January 6, 2022.

McCann, Frank. "The Ghost Dance, Last Hope of Western Tribes, Unleashed the Final Tragedy."

Montana: The Magazine of Western History 16 (1), Winter 1966. 25-34.

Mooney, James. "The Messiah Letter from Wovoka." Ghost Dance USA. ghostdance.us/history-messiah-letter.html/. Accessed January 8, 2022.

Moses, L. G. " 'The Father Tells Me So!' Wovoka, the Ghost Dance Prophet." *American Indian Quarterly* 9 (3), Summer 1985. 335-51.

New World Encyclopedia. "Wovoka." newworldencuclopedia.org/entry/Wovoka/. Accessed January 6, 2022.

Ostler, Jeffrey. "Conquest and the State: Why the United States Employed Massive Force to Suppress the Lakota Ghost Dance." *Pacific Historical Review* 65 (2), May 1996. 217-48.

Reilly, Hugh. "The 'Savage Dance of Death.' The Omaha Newspapers' Coverage of the Ghost Dance, 1890-91." *Heritage of the Great Plains* 36 (2), Fall-Winter 2012. esirc. emporia.edu/bitstream/handle/123456789/Reilly/. Accessed January 7, 2022.

Smoak, Gregory. "The Mormons and the Ghost Dance of 1890." *South Dakota Historical Society Quarterly* 16 (3), Fall 1986. 269-294.

Stillman, Deann. "The Unlikely Alliance Between Buffalo Bill and Sitting Bull." History.com, September 4, 2018. History.com/news/the-unlikely-alliance-between-buffalo-bill-and-sitting-bull/. Accessed January 11, 2022.

University of Michigan Library. "Great American Chiefs: Wovoka." apps.lib.umich.edu/online-exhibits/show/great-american-chiefs-wovoka/. Accessed January 6, 2022.

Warren, Louis. "Wounded Knee and the Ghost Dance: Christian Prayer, American Politics, and Indian Protest." *Reviews on American History* 39 (4), December 2011. 665-72.

Free Books by Charles River Editors

We have brand new titles available for free most days of the week. To see which of our titles are currently free, click on this link.

Discounted Books by Charles River Editors

We have titles at a discount price of just 99 cents each day. To see which of our titles are currently 99 cents, click on this link.